The descendants of George Little, who came to Newbury, Massachusetts, in 1640

George Thomas Little

Genealogy of the Little Family.

Descendants

OF

GEORGE LITTLE,

WHO CAME TO

Newbury, Massachusetts, in 1640.

COMPILED BY GEORGE T. LITTLE.

CAMBRIDGE:

Printed at the University Press,

BY CHARLES J. LITTLE.

1877.

PREFACE.

HE compiler is only too well aware of the incompleteness which marks several parts of the following Genealogy. Being unable, however, at present, to supply these deficiencies, he has decided to have it published, knowing that when printed the information it contains is less liable to be lost, and hoping that some one fitted for the task may be led to prepare a more extended account of the family. The abbreviations which occur are those used in genealogical works, and need no explanation. The figure at the right of the Christian name denotes the generation; e. g. Moses' shows that the grandson of George Little is referred to, and he is thus distinguished from his father and his son, who both had the same name. In order to avoid confusion it has sometimes been necessary to add the names of a person's father and grandfather, which are enclosed in brackets. The colored plate of the coat of arms is copied from an old painting belonging to the estate of the late Miss Hannah Little of Newburyport, which has been in the possession of her family for over a hundred years. The exact authority for the use of these "arms" is not known, but Guillim gives two or more families of the name of Little bearing the Saltier (or St. Andrew's cross) on the shield, though of different tinctures, in one of which they are simply reversed. In the

Appendix, at the close of the Genealogy, a few letters have been printed, which it is thought may be of interest to members of the family.

The facts contained in the following pages have been gathered from so many sources that it is hardly possible to mention all; but the writer is under special obligations to Messrs. William and Eben Little of Newbury, Dr. J. L. Hale of Boston, Benjamin Hale, Esq. of Newburyport, and Mr. C. J. Little of Cambridge.

George Little.

GEORGE LITTLE, the founder of the Newbury family of that name, came from Unicorn Street, near London Bridge, to Newbury, Massachusetts, in 1640. Though a young man, he appears to have been quite wealthy for those times, and made extensive purchases of lands. The farms of his selection are said to contain some of the finest land in the town, and have, with hardly an exception, remained in the hands of his direct descendants to the present time. He must have sustained a high reputation for ability and honesty, for we find him appointed the executor of several estates. In the prolonged ecclesiastical dispute which divided the church at Newbury for so many years he upheld the side of the pastor, Rev. Mr. Parker, but soon after the settling of the difficulties joined the first Baptist Church in Boston, and in 1682 became one of the members of a small church of the same denomination in his own town. Though not an educated man, he was remarkable for his strength of mind as well as of body. The following letter, written to him by an acquaintance, is appended as an example of the correspondence of that day, and more particularly to show the way in which his surname was frequently spelled : —

Dear & loving brother littell, in gospell bonds be my harty love rememered unto you, and unto your wife though unto me unknown, & hoping you are in helth as I being att this wrighting hereof. blessed be the Lord, hartily giving you thanks for your kind entertainment when I was last at your house. This is farther to let you understand I have married to one Margery Colman a widdow on the island Nantucket where I now am. [Here follows an announcement of various other matters of no particular interest.] Committing you to the protection of the Almighty God & begging your & all my brethrens' prayers for my being [   ] into his heavenly kingdom & delivered from every sinful way & work I rest your loving brother

THOMAS OSBURNE.

NANTUCKET ISLAND
This 25 of the 8 month 1682.

Superscription : This for his very loving frend
Goodman Littell living att Newbury
Deliver this with care I pray.

Rev. Daniel Little.

EV. DANIEL LITTLE of Wells, one of the
most eminent and influential of the clergy-
men in Maine during the last century, was
born in Newburyport July 18, 1724. Though
he never enjoyed the advantages of a collegiate education, his mental powers were strengthened and trained
by several years of teaching, and the degree of A. M.
was conferred upon him in 1766 by Harvard College.
He studied theology with Rev. Joseph Moody of York,
and in March of 1751 he was ordained pastor of the
second parish in Wells, a position which he occupied
until his death, over fifty years later. His pastoral
duties were faithfully and successfully performed. He
was deeply interested in the temporal as well as spir-
itual welfare of his parishioners, and was always em-
ployed in devising some means for its promotion.
None but the kindest feelings were exercised towards
him by his people during the remarkably long term of
years he was their minister.

In 1772 he was appointed for missionary service in
the eastern portion of the District of Maine. This led,
during the course of the following years, to a series of

degree arduous. The success which attended
however, was fully sufficient to justify them,
came to be styled the Apostle of the East. On
casion he was sent especially to the Indians on
nobscot, and established a school for them,
was quite successful until the interference of
tholic priests, who discouraged the undertaking.
time he took an opportunity to learn the lan-
and afterwards prepared a full vocabulary.
ghout his life he manifested much interest in the
ion of the young, and though then far advanced
s, was selected as one of the trustees of Bow-
ollege at its establishment. He died suddenly
lysis, on the 5th of December, 1801, leaving
children and grandchildren. One of the latter,
s, afterwards became the leading partner in the
Little, Brown, & Co., Boston.

NEWBURYPORT, FROM POWOW HILL.

Colonel Moses Little.

COLONEL MOSES LITTLE was a man remarkable for his energy of body as well as of mind. His younger years were devoted to the settling of wild lands in the neighboring provinces. About 1750, in company with one or two others, he obtained from Governor Benning Wentworth a large grant of the unoccupied crown lands lying within the present limits of Vermont. A few years later he purchased a large interest in the township of Apthorp, New Hampshire, which was afterwards divided, one town being named in his honor Littleton, and the other Dalton, from his townsman, Hon. Tristram Dalton. His possessions in this region were increased to a great extent by subsequent purchases. In the mean time, together with Major Samuel Gerrish and Colonel Jonathan Bagley, he acted as agent for the proprietors of Bakerstown, and succeeded in obtaining for them from the General Court of Massachusetts a township of land in Maine in lieu of the one granted in 1736, which was subsequently decided to be within the borders of New Hampshire. By purchasing from time to time the rights of the original proprietors he became the owner of the greater part of the grant, which comprised a large and valuable portion of what is now Androscoggin County. In 1768 the Pejepscot Company granted him and Colonel Bagley a still larger tract in the same county, but on the eastern side of the Androscoggin, on condition that they would settle fifty families there before June 1, 1774, and build certain roads. The conditions, we believe, were only partially fulfilled, and the amount of land actually deeded was somewhat diminished in consequence.

The war of the Revolution found Colonel Little over fifty years of age, but as active and earnest in the defence of his country's liberties as the youngest. Upon the first tidings of the encounter at Lexington he raised a company and marched to the American headquarters at Cambridge. At the battle of Bunker Hill he was in command of a regiment, led his men across Charlestown Neck under a terrible fire from the British batteries and ships of war, and arrived at the scene of action just before the third and final charge of the enemy. He assisted in covering the retreat from the hill. Though unwounded, he had several narrow escapes, men on each side of him being killed, and his clothes bespattered with blood. Called home in August to attend the funeral of two of his children, he rejoined his command after an absence of only two days. He went with the army to New York after the evacuation of Boston, and was present at the disastrous engagement on Long Island. For a month or two subsequently he was intrusted with the command of an encampment at Peekskill, but joined his commander-in-chief in time to take part in the battles of Trenton and Princeton. Early in 1777 he was obliged, on account of ill health, to return home, and two years later, for the same reason, to decline the command of a naval armament raised by the Commonwealth to dislodge the enemy from their position on the Penobscot. He lost his speech in 1781 by a stroke of paralysis. He was characterized by imperturbable self-possession, and an acute knowledge of human nature. Early in the war he became acquainted with Washington, who held him in high esteem, and often relied upon his judgment. An autograph letter from the latter, together with the sword worn at the battle of Bunker Hill, and other relics, are still in the possession of his descendants at Newbury.

George Little.

EORGE LITTLE[1] came from London to Newbury in 1640. He married Alice Poore, who sailed for New England from Southampton in May, 1638, together with her younger brothers Samuel and Daniel, in the party of Mr. Richard Dummer. She died 1 Dec., 1680, aged 62. His second wife was Eleanor Barnard, widow of Thomas Barnard of Amesbury, whom he married 19 July, 1681, and who survived him, dying 27 Nov., 1694. The exact time of his death is not known, but it was between 15 March, 1693, and 27 Nov., 1694. He had five children:—

    I. Sarah, born 8 May, 1652; died 19 Nov., 1652.
    II. Capt. Joseph, born 22 Sept., 1653; died 6 Sept., 1740.
    III. John, born 28 July, 1655; died 20 July, 1672.
    IV. Moses, born 11 March, 1657; died 8 March, 1691.
    V. Sarah, born 24 Nov., 1661.

Capt. Joseph[2] married Mary, daughter of Tristram Coffin, Esq., 31 Oct., 1677. She died 28 Nov., 1725, in her 69th year. Their children were:—

  I. Judith, born 19 July, 1678.

  II. Joseph, born 23 Feb., 1680 ; died 14 Aug., 1693.

  III. George, born 12 Jan., 1682.

  IV. Sarah, born 23 Oct., 1683.

  V. Enoch, born 9 Dec., 1685 ; died 28 April, 1766.

  VI. Tristram, born 7 April, 1688 ; died April, 1762.

  VII. Moses, born 5 May, 1690 ; died 15 Aug., 1725.

 VIII. Daniel, born 13 Jan., 1692.

  IX. Benjamin, born 27 Dec., 1693 ; died Feb., 1737.

Moses[2] married Lydia, daughter of Tristram and Judith Coffin. His estate was returned to Probate Court 3 Nov., 1691, as amounting to £1065.6. Their children were :—

  I. John, born 8 Jan., 1680 ; died unmarried, 25 March, 1753.

  II. Tristram, born 9 Dec., 1681 ; died 11 Nov., 1765.

  III. Sarah, born 28 April, 1684 ; married Thomas Pike 3 Jan., 1710, and died 10 Dec., 1710.

  IV. Mary, born 13 Jan., 1686 ; married Joseph, son of Mr. Moses Gerrish, 26 Feb., 1703.

  V. Elizabeth, born 25 May, 1688 ; married Anthony Morse 21 Jan., 1718, and died 17 March, 1719.

  VI. Moses, born 26 Feb., 1691 ; died 17 Oct., 1780.

Sarah[2] was married 3 March, 1682, to Joseph Ilsley, son of William Ilsley, a yeoman from Wiltshire, England.   Their children were : —

  I.   Mary, born 20 Jan., 1683.
  II. Joseph, born 14 Aug., 1684.
  III. Lydia, born 15 June, 1687.
  IV. Sarah, born 16 July, 1689.

George[2] married Edna, daughter of Capt. Thomas Hale, 22 Feb., 1711.   Their children were : —

  I.   Thomas, born 27 Oct., 1711, and married Mary Bond of Haverhill, 12 Jan., 1738.
  II. ——————, born and died 25 Sept., 1712.
  III. George, born 9 Sept., 1713 ; married, 30 July, 1734, Mary Kimball, who died 20 July, 1743. He then married Elizabeth Poor of Rowley, 29 May, 1754.
  IV. ——————, born and died 25 March, 1715.
  V.   Oliver, born 8 Sept., 1716 ; died 9 Oct., 1716.
  VI. Edna, born 21 Aug., 1717.
  VII. Alice, born 27 April, 1719.
  VIII. Ezekiel, born 6 March, 1721.
  IX. Bartholomew, born 10 March, 1725 ; died 10 May, 1725.
  X.   Joseph, born 22 June, 1727.

Sarah[3] [Joseph[2]] was married, 14 Jan., 1703, to John Kent, who was born 16 July, 1675, and died 24 March,

1704. They had no children. She then married Bartholomew Thing of Exeter, 2 April, 1712, and after his death John Downing.

Ensign Enoch[3] married, 19 May, 1707, Elizabeth, daughter of John Worth. He was one of the first settlers in West Newbury, and lived on Crane-Neck Hill. His children were: —

    I. Joseph, born 3 July, 1708; died in childhood.
   II. Elizabeth, born 21 Jan., 1711; married Abel Huse, Jr., 29 April, 1729.
  III. John, born 22 March, 1713; died 4 Aug., 1730.
  IV. Capt. Edmund, born 5 Sept., 1715; married Judith Adams 18 March, 1736, and died 29 Aug., 1803.
   V. Enoch, born 30 April, 1718; died young.
  VI. Daniel, born 4 May, 1726; died 2 Feb., 1730.
 VII. Benjamin, born April, 1729; died young.

Tristram[3] [Joseph[2]] married Anna, daughter of Stephen Emery, 10 April, 1711. His wife died 4 Oct., 1755, aged 62 years. Their children were: —

    I. Mary, born 17 March, 1713; married Capt. Michael Dalton 5 Feb., 1734.
   II. Stephen, born 31 March, 1715; died 11 Nov., 1716.

III. Anna, born 4 Aug., 1716; married Stephen
Sewall 27 Dec., 1739; died 16 Feb., 1796.

IV. Judith, born 22 Sept., 1720; died unmarried
11 Feb., 1796.

V. Sarah, born 8 Aug., 1724; died 26 Nov., 1736.

VI. Abigail, born 21 Nov., 1730; died 20 Aug., 1736.

RISTRAM DALTON, son of Capt. Michael
Dalton and Mary Little, was born in Newburyport, 28 May, 1738, and graduated at
Harvard University at the early age of 17.
He studied law as an accomplishment, the fortune
which he inherited from his father not requiring
him to practise it as a profession, and he took a
deep interest in the cultivation of a large landed
estate in what is now the town of West Newbury.
Washington, John Adams, Louis Philippe, Talleyrand,
and other distinguished guests partook of his hospi-
talities. As eminent for piety as he was for mental
endowments, the Episcopal Church, of which he was a
warden, shared in his generous liberality. He was a
Representative, Speaker of the House of Representatives, and a Senator in the Legislature of Massachusetts, and a Senator of the United States in the first
Congress after the adoption of the Federal Constitution. When Washington City was founded Mr. Dal-

ton invested his entire fortune in lands there, and lost it by the mismanagement of a business agent. At the same time a vessel which was freighted with his furniture and valuable library was lost on her voyage from Newburyport to Washington, and he thus found himself, after having lived sixty years in affluence, penniless. Several offices of profit and honor were immediately tendered him by the government, and he accepted the Surveyorship of Boston. He died in Boston 30 May, 1817, and his remains were taken to Newburyport, where they were interred in the burial-ground of St. Paul's Church.

Moses [Joseph] married, 5 Jan., 1715, Mary, daughter of Capt. Thomas Hale. Their children were :—

I. Ebenezer, born 18 Oct., 1715 ; married Elizabeth Brown 5 April, 1737 ; died 30 July, 1768.

II. Nathan, born 12 May, 1717 ; married Hannah Mighill of Rowley, 12 Nov., 1741 ; died 1745.

III. Sarah, born 27 Feb., 1718 ; married Parker Titcomb 11 Oct., 1737.

IV. Mary, born 16 Aug., 1720 ; married John Berry 20 Feb., 1741.

V. Hannah, born 13 June, 1722 ; married Joseph Low 15 Jan., 1747.

VI. Elizabeth, born 30 Dec., 1723 ; married John Frazer 26 July, 1743.

VII. Moses, born 9 Feb., 1725.

Daniel [Joseph²] married Abiah Clement 1712.
Their children were : —

    I. Samuel, born in Newbury 23 April, 1714 ; married Hannah Sewall 1736.
    II. Joseph, born in Newbury 6 Nov., 1715.
    III. Sarah, born in Haverhill 11 Nov., 1717.
    IV. Elizabeth, born in Haverhill 12 Nov., 1719.
    V. Mary, born in Haverhill 6 Oct., 1721.
    VI. Abiah, born in Haverhill 14 Aug., 1723.
    VII. Rev. Daniel, born 18 July, 1724 ; married in 1751 Mary, daughter of Rev. Joseph Emerson, who died 2 June, 1758, aged 32, and Sarah Coffin 6 June, 1759 ; died 5 Dec., 1801.
    VIII. Hannah, born 21 Jan., 1726 ; died 7 Sept., 1726.
    IX. Judith, born 11 July, 1727 ; died 6 Aug., 1727.
    X. Ruth, born 14 Sept., 1728.
    XI. Abigail, born 19 Jan., 1730 ; died 14 April, 1737.

Tristram [Moses²] married Sarah, daughter of
Henry and Sarah Dole, 30 Oct., 1707. Their children were : —

    I. Sarah, born 6 Aug., 1708 ; married James Noyes 30 May, 1729, and lived in Atkinson, N. H.

II. Henry, born 31 Dec., 1710; married Lydia Little 7 Dec., 1738; died Dec., 1786.

III. Samuel, born 18 Feb., 1713; married Dorothy Noyes 18 Feb., 1736; lived in Atkinson, N. H., and died 29 Sept., 1792.

IV. Apphia, baptized 1715; died 15 Feb., 1743.

V. Jane, born 6 June, 1718; married Edmund Knight 25 May, 1741.

VI. Elizabeth, born 20 Nov., 1720; married Humphrey Noyes 22 Nov., 1743; lived in Atkinson, N. H., and died 15 April, 1818.

VII. Nathaniel, born 24 May, 1723; died before Louisburg, C. B., 13 Nov., 1745.

VIII. Richard, born 6 June, 1725; married Jane Noyes 17 Sept., 1754; died 13 Feb., 1806.

IX. Enoch, born 21 May, 1728; married Sarah Pettingill 19 Feb., 1755, Hannah Hovey 5 June, 1759; lived in Boscawen, N. H.; died 21 Oct., 1816.

X. Mary, born 4 Feb., 1731; died young.

XI. John, born 14 July, 1735; married Hannah Noyes 27 Oct., 1767; died 25 Aug., 1800.

Moses[3] [Moses[2]] married Sarah, daughter of Sergeant Stephen and Deborah Jacques, 12 Feb., 1716. She was born 23 Sept., 1697, and died 11 Nov. 1763.

The following epitaph is taken from a stone in the
Upper Burying-Ground on the Plains at Newbury:—

Mr. Moses Little departed this life Oct
17th 1780 in the 90th year of his Age
He was temperate in all things
Industrious, hospitable yet frugal
A kind husband and tender father
A good neighbor & good citizen
and while living justly sustained the first
of Characters — an honest man.

" A wit's a feather a chief's a rod
An honest man's ye noblest work of God."

His children were : —

I. Lydia, born 25 Aug., 1717 ; married Henry
Little 7 Dec., 1738 ; died 4 Feb., 1798.

II. Stephen, born 19 May, 1719 ; died 30 Aug.,
1793.

III. John, born 16 Nov., 1721 ; married Temper-
ance Ripp 14 May, 1745, and died 9 May,
1799.

IV. Moses, born 8 May, 1724 ; died 27 May, 1798.

V. Joseph, born 29 May, 1726 ; died 26 Jan., 1727.

VI. Sarah, born 17 Feb., 1728 ; died 30 March,
1728.

VII. Joseph, born 21 April, 1730 ; married Elizabeth
Hazen ; died 1 Feb., 1792.

VIII. Benjamin, born 4 Nov., 1732; married Mary
      Hazen; died 1777.

IX. Sarah, born 8 April, 1735; married William
      Pottle of Stratham, N. H., 4 May, 1758.

X. Mary, born 25 Oct., 1737; married Jonathan
      Wiggin of Stratham, N. H., Oct., 1761; died
      14 Aug., 1771.

XI. Paul, born 1 April, 1740; died 11 Feb., 1818.

XII. Elizabeth, born 16 Oct., 1742; died 16 April,
      1753.

Deacon Stephen[4] [Moses[3] Moses[2]] married, 5 Aug.,
1743, Judith Bailey, who died 1764, aged 40, and afterwards Mary Long, who survived him, dying 1798, in
her 75th year. Their youngest child, Jacob[5], born 1763,
married Hannah, daughter of Moses and Hannah Sawyer, 28 Sept., 1786. Their children were:—

I. Mary, born 30 May, 1788; married, 13 Oct.,
      1811, Reuben Fisher.

II. Infant son,)   died 19 Nov., 1789.
              twins, born 18 Nov., 1789.

III. Infant son,)   died 20 Nov., 1789.

IV. Moses Sawyer, born 28 Sept., 1790; married
      widow Henrietta Perkins.

V. Hannah, born 18 May, 1792; died unmarried
      16 Oct., 1876.

VI. Judith, born 20 April, 1795.

VII. Jacob, born 19 March, 1797, in Newburyport,
    Mass.   He was one of the most prominent
    of New York brokers.

THRIFT, forecast, and industry distinguished
his ancestry, and the archives of the family
are stored with precious relics of the patri-
otism of the founders of the line.   His father,
Jacob Little, was a man of large wealth and distinction.
But disaster, that comes sooner or later to nearly every
mercantile house, swept away his property, and the
war of 1812 nearly completed his financial ruin.

Jacob inherited from his ancestry a sound constitution, good principles, and indomitable energy.   His
father as a merchant had transacted business with the
leading merchants, and among them was well acquainted with the renowned Jacob Barker, and had no
difficulty in securing a place for his son in Mr. Barker's
counting-house.   In 1817 he entered Mr. Barker's service, and at once became a favorite with that shrewd
and successful merchant.   Having remained here five
years and completed his apprenticeship, he in 1822
selected a small basement office on Wall Street, and
began business on his own account as an exchange
specie broker.   During the next twelve years — work-
ing eighteen hours a day in his little office — he

promptly and shrewdly executed all orders ; and his success was due no less to his integrity than to his talent.

In 1834 Mr. Little stood at the head of the leading financiers and bankers of the city. He controlled large amounts of stock and money, and was known as the " Napoleon of the board." But, however wise or prudent, shrewd or gifted with forecast a man may be, however large or well invested his fortune, *if he is a speculator* he cannot be sure that commercial disaster will not overtake him. Mr. Little did not escape. Thrice he was carried down, but he was never dishonored. He recovered himself, and paid up his contracts in full ; on his first suspension, though legally free from liability, he disbursed nearly $ 1,000,000, paying every creditor in full with interest ; so that it was a common saying among moneyed men. that Jacob Little's suspended paper was better than the checks of most merchants. He closed his long career without a stain upon his mercantile reputation.

He died 28 March, 1865, leaving a widow and one son. The news of his death startled the great city. Merchants congregated to do him honor. Resolutions of enduring respect were adopted, and the Stock Board adjourned to attend his funeral. He was borne to his burial (in Greenwood Cemetery) with all honor.

VIII. William, born 6 Feb., 1799; died young.

IX. Alfred, born 16 Dec., 1802; died young.

X. Edward Bass, born 3 July, 1804; an eminent banker of New York City.

XI. Caroline, born 12 Jan., 1806; married John Phillips.

XII. Harriet, born 5 Aug., 1808.

Paul[4] [Moses[3] Moses[2]] married, 20 May, 1762, Hannah Emery, who died Sept., 1771; Widow Sarah Souther of Ipswich, 30 Aug., 1772, who died 26 Sept., 1797, aged 54; and afterwards widow Sarah Emerson of Boxford, who died 25 May, 1817, aged 55. He moved from Newburyport to Portland in 1761; was a goldsmith by trade, but engaged in commercial business to a considerable extent. After the destruction of the town by the British in 1776, he removed to Windham, where many of his descendants still reside. His children are : —

I. Hannah, born April, 1764; married Emery of Newbury.

II. Paul, Jr., born April, 1767; died Jan., 1850.

III. Mary, born Sept., 1775; died Nov., 1787.

IV. Dr. Timothy, born 27 Oct., 1776; died 27 Nov., 1849.

V. Moses, born Jan., 1782; died 1866.

VI. Thomas, born 1788 ; died 1856.

VII. Sarah, born 25 March, 1802.

Dr. Timothy[5] [Paul[4] Moses[3]], a prominent physician and citizen of Portland, married Elizabeth Lowell 12 Oct., 1806. Their children were :—

 I. Haller, born 3 May, 1807 ; died 19 May, 1876.

 II. Capt. John L., born 13 April, 1809 ; married, 15 Sept., 1835, Susan W. Walker of Kennebunkport.

 III. William W., died young.

 IV. Lowell, died young.

 V. Charles H., born 9 Aug., 1817 ; married Mary D. Whorf 14 Sept., 1845.

Moses[5] [Paul[4] Moses[3]] married, 7 Oct., 1819, Hannah Horton of Portland, who survives him. Their children are :—

 I. Henry Augustus, born July, 1820 ; died April, 1827.

 II. Abba Horton, born April, 1822.

 III. William Pitt Fessenden, born Dec., 1824 ; died Dec., 1845.

 IV. Moses Henry, born May, 1829.

 V. Sarah Norton, born June, 1831 ; died Oct., 1848.

 VI. Augustus Horton, born Dec., 1833 ; died July, 1862.

Sarah[5] [Paul[4] Moses[3]] married, 6 Jan., 1825, Oliver Gerrish, a leading jeweller of Portland. Their children are:—

I. An infant daughter, died at birth.
II. Sarah Caroline, born 11 April, 1830.
III. Charles Oliver, born 19 March, 1834; married, 19 March, 1867, Julia P. Jordan.
IV. William Little, born 31 Aug., 1841; graduated at Bowdoin 1864, entered U. S. Army, promoted to 2d Lieutenant, died before Petersburg, Va., 11 Feb., 1865.
V. Frederic Henry, born 21 March, 1845; graduated at Bowdoin 1866, and from Maine Medical School 1869, where he is Professor of Materia Medica and Therapeutics.

The remaining pages contain only the names of the descendants of Col. Moses and Abigail Little.

COL. MOSES[4] [Moses[3] Moses[2]] married, 5 June, 1743, Abigail, daughter of Joshua Bailey, twin-sister of Judith, who married his brother Stephen, also sister of Gen. Jacob Bailey, a distinguished officer in the French and Revolutionary wars. She died 6 Feb., 1815, aged 91. Their children were:—

I. Sarah, born 15 Dec., 1743 ; died 14 Aug., 1775.

II. Michael, born 9 Jan., 1746 ; died 13 Feb., 1746.

III. Josiah, born 16 Feb., 1747 ; died 26 Dec., 1830.

IV. Abigail, born 2 April, 1749 ; died 20 Sept., 1838.

V. Lydia, born 24 Nov., 1751 ; died 19 Sept., 1820.

VI. Elizabeth, born 3 Sept., 1754 ; died 22 Feb., 1792.

VII. Anna, born 20 March, 1757 ; died 13 Aug., 1775.

VIII. Mary, born 22 Sept., 1759 ; died 28 Aug., 1847.

IX. Hannah, born 21 May, 1762 ; died 25 Nov., 1849.

X. Alice, born 10 May, 1764 ; died 6 May, 1765.

XI. Moses, born 20 Jan., 1767 ; died 28 April, 1857.

Sarah[5] [Moses[4] Moses[3] Moses[2]] was married 19 June, 1765, to John Noyes, who died of small-pox on Kent's Island, Newbury, 18 July, 1778. Their children were : —

I. Infant son, born and died 1776.

II. Abigail, born 16 March, 1767 ; died 5 Aug., 1842.

III. Daniel, born 26 Feb., 1769; died 17 April,
    1774.

IV. Sarah, born 25 Oct., 1771; died 31 March,
    1776.

V. Elizabeth, born 18 Aug., 1773; died 7 April,
    1775.

Abigail Noyes[6] [Sarah[5] Moses[4]] married, 24 March,
1785, David, son of Stephen[4] Little. They lived in
Newbury. Their children were :—

I. John Noyes, born 26 Sept., 1786; died unmar-
    ried 27 Jan., 1810.

II. Sarah, born 29 Sept., 1790; died 14 May, 1863.

III. Mary, born 22 May, 1793; died unmarried 20
    March, 1826.

IV. Stephen William, born 10 Dec., 1795.

V. Abigail, born 5 Dec., 1797; died 30 Oct., 1865.

VI. Ebenezer, born 9 Feb., 1801.

VII. Elizabeth, born 22 April, 1805; died 12 Dec.,
    1869.

Sarah[7] [Abigail[6] Sarah[5] Moses[4]] married, 5 Dec.,
1815, Tristram[6] [Nathaniel[5] Henry[4]] Little. Their
children were :—

I. Abigail Noyes, born 8 Sept., 1816; died 2 June,
    1871.

II. Nathaniel, born 24 Sept., 1818.

III. Mary Toppan, born 23 Jan., 1821.

IV. David, born 7 Jan., 1823 ; died at sea 16 June, 1852.

V. William, born 14 Oct., 1825.

VI. Elizabeth, born 7 Feb., 1828.

VII. Sarah, born 26 May, 1830 ; died 13 May, 1857.

III. George, born 10 July, 1832 ; died 28 July, 1832.

IX. Alfred, born 9 May, 1834.

Nathaniel [Sarah Abigail Sarah Moses] married May, 1845, Mary P. Danforth. Their children are : —

I. Alice Archer, born 19 Aug., 1846.

II. Heber, born 18 Nov., 1853.

William [Sarah Abigail Sarah Moses] married, Oct., 1864, Ellen M., daughter of John and Mary J. Chapman] Carleton of Haverhill, Mass. Their children are : —

I. Sarah, born 27 July, 1865 ; died 5 Jan., 1876.

II. Carleton, born 10 Dec., 1866.

III. George, born 15 July, 1868.

IV. William Toppan, born 2 April, 1870 ; died 22 Dec., 1875.

V. Abby Noyes, born 5 Jan., 1872.

VI. John Chapman, born 30 Sept., 1873 ; died 29 Dec., 1875.

VII. Margaret Whittier, born 10 Dec., 1874; died
24 Aug., 1875.

Elizabeth⁸ [Sarah⁷ Abigail⁶ Sarah⁵ Moses⁴] married,
12 Sept., 1850, Nathan N., son of Rev. Leonard and
Caroline [Noyes] Withington.   Their children are: —

I. Infant son, born and died 12 Nov., 1851.
II. Infant son, born and died 11 July, 1852.
III. David Little, born 2 Feb., 1854.
IV. Lothrop, born 31 Jan., 1856.
V. Mary Noyes, born 20 Feb., 1859.
VI. Anne Toppan, born 17 Jan., 1867.
VII. Arthur Amos, born 9 Feb., 1869.

Stephen William⁷ [Abigail⁶ Sarah⁵ Moses⁴] married,
16 May, 1820, Hannah M., daughter of William and
Judith [Killam] Russell.   Their children are: —

I. Infant son, born and died 1 April, 1821.
II. John Noyes, born 29 Jan., 1822; died 31 May,
1823.
III. Lucy Maria, born 22 March, 1824; died 14
Oct., 1824.
IV. Mary Jane, born 29 Sept., 1825; died 18 Aug.,
1832.
V. Isaac Warren, born 9 Nov., 1826.
VI. William Russell, born 5 July, 1828; died 1 Oct.,
1830.

VII. Susan Caroline, born 24 May, 1830 ; died Sept., 1859.
VIII. Stephen William, born 17 July, 1831.
IX. Lucy Jane, born 10 April, 1833.
X. Hannah Mary, born 1 Jan., 1835.

Isaac Warren[8] [Stephen W.[7] Abigail[6] Sarah[5] Moses[4]] married, 7 May, 1854, Abigail P., daughter of Daniel and Elizabeth [Donnell] Brown. Their children are:—

I. Ada Brooks, born 5 May, 1856.
II. Edith Brown, born 12 Oct., 1859.
III. Sumner Scott, born 29 Jan., 1866.
IV. Laura Warren, born 27 June, 1868.
V. Fanny Ellen, born 17 Oct., 1872.

Stephen William[8] [Stephen W.[7] Abigail[6] Sarah[5] Moses[4]] married, 11 Oct., 1854, Mary, daughter of Joseph and Elizabeth [Moody] Little. Their children are :

I. Infant son, born and died 3 Sept., 1855.
II. Russell Moody, born 7 May, 1858.
III. Susan Caroline, born 4 June, 1862.
IV. Lyman Cushing, born 16 Nov., 1866.

Hannah Mary[8] [Stephen W.[7] Abigail[6] Sarah[5] Moses[4]] married, 19 Aug., 1853, Henry S., son of Sewall and Sarah [Ilsley] Adams. Their children are:—

I. Agnes Little, born 4 Sept., 1854.

   II. Emily Judson, born 23 Sept., 1856.

  III. Norman Ilsley, born 16 Feb., 1864.

  IV. Henrietta Sewall, born 1 Aug., 1867.

   V. Howard Shirley, born 14 April, 1870.

  VI. Wesley Irving, born 29 Dec., 1871.

Abigail[7] [Abigail[6] Sarah[5] Moses[4]] married Richard, son of Asa and Dolly [Morse] Adams, 30 April, 1821. Their children are : —

    I. Giles Aaron, born 31 March, 1822.

   II. Mary Little, born 20 Sept., 1823.

  III. Asa, born 1 Nov., 1824.

  IV. Calvin, born 23 May, 1827 ; died 16 Jan., 1831.

   V. Rufus, born 31 March, 1829.

  VI. Elizabeth Noyes, born 24 Feb., 1831.

 VII. Annie Rolfe, born 14 June, 1832.

VIII. Margaret Emery, born 3 Sept., 1833 ; died 30 Sept., 1871.

  IX. Richard Calvin, born 14 Dec., 1835 ; died 29 May, 1836.

   X. Susan Pike, born 24 Sept., 1838.

  XI. Richard, born 23 July, 1842 ; died 2 Sept., 1842.

Giles Aaron[8] [Abigail[7] Abigail[6] Sarah[5] Moses[4]] married, 12 Jan., 1848, Sarah E. Jackman, daughter of Moses and Harriet [Carr] Jackman. Their children are : —

I. Ellen Harriet, born 22 June, 1851.

II. Sarah Agnes, born 8 Jan., 1854.

III. Alice Morse, born 5 Nov., 1856; died 5 Feb., 1862.

IV. Richard Giles, born 29 Dec., 1858.

V. Nettie Carr, born 20 Aug., 1861; died 1 Feb., 1865.

VI. Carrie Little, born 2 Sept., 1864.

VII. Lizzie Carr, born 13 July, 1867.

VIII. Herbert Lawrence, born 23 March, 1872.

Mary L. Adams [Abigail⁵ Abigail⁴ Sarah³ Moses⁴] married, 28 April, 1847, Joseph Noyes Rolfe, son of Moses and Sarah Brown [Noyes] Rolfe. Their children are:—

I. Moses Henry, born 8 May, 1848.

II. Abbie Little, born 21 Dec., 1849; died 23 June, 1860.

III. John Calvin, born 29 Aug., 1851.

IV. Charles Greenleaf, born 27 Aug., 1853; died 1 Sept., 1857.

V. Helen Noyes, born 2 Oct., 1855.

VI. Charles Joseph, born 31 Aug., 1858.

VII. Willard Greenleaf, born 1 July, 1860.

VIII. Edward, born 8 June, 1862; died 9 June, 1862.

IX. Abbie Little, born 11 Aug., 1863.

X. Walter Lumbert, born 23 Aug., 1866; died 31 Aug., 1869.

Moses Henry Rolfe[9] [Mary L. Adams[8] Abigail[7] Abigail[6] Sarah[5]] married, 15 Jan., 1873, Abbie Frances, daughter of Daniel K. and Elizabeth [Pettingell] Hale. Their children are :—

    I. Mary Adams, born 27 March, 1874.

    II. Henry Pettingell, born 7 Sept., 1876.

Asa[8] [Abigail[7] Abigail[6] Sarah[5] Moses[4]] married, 1 July, 1857, Mary C., daughter of Daniel and Nancy [Pike] Colman.   Their children are :—

    I. Annie Colman, born 5 April, 1858 ; died 24 Oct., 1862.

    II. George Moulton, born 25 April, 1861.

    III. Daniel Colman, born 16 March, 1863 ; died Aug., 1865.

Rufus[8] [Abigail[7] Abigail[6] Sarah[5] Moses[4]] married, 6 Nov., 1855, Eunice Short, daughter of Major and Sarah [Pettingell] Goodwin.

Elizabeth Noyes[8] [Abigail[7] Abigail[6] Sarah[5] Moses[4]] married, 16 Sept., 1860, Anthony, son of Charles and Ann [Huse] Knapp.   Their children are :—

    I. Annie Florence, born 27 July, 1861.

    II. Henry Anthony, born 4 July, 1863.

    III. Sarah Richardson, born 25 June, 1867.

    IV. Margaret Gertrude, born 13 July, 1872.

Margaret Emery[5] [Abigail[7] Abigail[6] Sarah[5] Moses[4]] married, 4 July, 1857, George Washington, son of John Little and Elizabeth [Goodwin] Knight. Their children are : -

   I. John Little, born 15 Jan., 1859.
  II. George Edward, born Sept., 1862 ; died Sept., 1862.
 III. Lizzie Hoyt, born Feb., 1864 ; died Feb., 1865.
 IV. Abbie Florence, born 13 Sept., 1869.

Susan Pike[5] [Abigail[6] Abigail[6] Sarah[5] Moses[4]] married, March, 1859, Charles Leonard, son of Charles L. and Martha [Goodwin] Ayers. Their children are :—

   I. Charles William, born 30 Sept., 1863.
  II. Edward Russell, born 20 Feb., 1867.
 III. George Custer, born 17 Nov., 1876 ; died 18 Nov., 1876.

Ebenezer[5] [Abigail[6] Sarah[5] Moses[4]] married, 30 Dec., 1822, Eliza, daughter of Ebenezer and Edna Adams. Their children are :—

   I. Catherine Adams, born 16 Sept., 1823.
  II. Daniel Noyes, born 15 Jan., 1826 ; died 10 Jan., 1831.
 III. George F., born 6 July, 1828 ; died 26 Jan., 1831.

   IV. Sarah Noyes, born 7 Aug., 1830 ; died 4 March, 1847.

   V. George F., born 24 March, 1832.

   VI. Edna Adams,   ⎫   died 2 June, 1839.

                ⎬ twins, born 2 June, 1834.

  VII. Abigail Noyes, ⎭   died 9 June, 1834.

VIII. Daniel Noyes, born 8 March, 1836 ; died 8 Dec., 1858.

   IX. Ebenezer, born 29 Sept., 1841.

   X. Sarah Eliza, born 1 Feb., 1853 ; married Edwin C., son of Rev. Elbridge G. Little, 10 June, 1873 ; died 5 May, 1875.

Catharine A.[3] [Ebenezer[7] Abigail[6] Sarah[5] Moses[4]] married, 21 March, 1850, Edward H., son of Henry and Phebe [Little] Little. Their children are : —

   I. Henry Bailey, born 3 Jan., 1851.

  II. Edward Francis, born 9 Feb. 1853.

 III. William White, born 18 Feb., 1856 ; died 25 June, 1857.

  IV. Daniel Noyes, born 16 Oct., 1858.

   V. Eliza Adams, born 9 Jan., 1861.

George F.[2] [Ebenezer[7] Abigail[6] Sarah[5] Moses[4]] married, 2 Feb., 1854, Alice, daughter of Henry and Phebe [Little] Little. Their children are : —

   I. Helen Maria, born 4 Jan., 1855.

  II. Caroline, born 19 May, 1857.

    III. Millard, born 17 Oct., 1858.

    IV. George Irving, born 27 Oct., 1860.

    V. Frank Wilbur, born 20 June, 1862.

    VI. Henry Alden, born 28 Nov., 1863.

    VII. Preston, born 10 July, 1865.

    VIII. Eben Sherman, born 3 May, 1867.

    IX. Walter Everett, born 2 April, 1869.

    X. Charles Herbert, born 5 Jan., 1874.

    XI. Catharine Alice, born 19 July, 1875.

Eben [Ebenezer Abigail Sarah Moses] married Lucy A., daughter of Daniel D. and Lucy G. [Pettingell] Greenleaf. Their only child is Henry Willard, born 17 July, 1865.

Elizabeth [Abigail Sarah Moses] married 11 March, 1823, Samuel, son of Samuel and Eunice McIntire Brookings. Their children are : —

    I. Eunice McIntire, born 4 Feb., 1824.

    II. John Bagley, born 12 June, 1826.

    III. David Little, born 5 Aug., 1828.

    IV. Melvin Fessenden, born 23 Dec., 1830.

    V. George William, born 17 Sept., 1833.

    VI. Elizabeth Sarah, born 5 Dec., 1835.

    VII. Mary Little, born 15 Aug., 1839 ; died 12 March, 1844.

    VIII. Samuel, born 24 Aug., 1841.

    IX. Philip, born 4 Sept., 1843 ; died 13 Jan., 1845.

COL. JOSIAH[5] [Moses[4] Moses[3]] married, 23 Nov., 1770. Sarah, daughter of Edward Toppan of Newbury. She was born 27 May, 1748, and died 11 Oct., 1823.

Col. Josiah Little, like his father, was a man of wonderful energy and activity. Every year, until he was nearly eighty, it was his custom to visit his lands in Maine, New Hampshire, and Vermont, driving over the rough roads alone, even after he had lost one hand by a premature explosion while overseeing the blasting of a passage through some rapids on the Androscoggin. He had charge of his father's real estate for many years, and early gained an acquaintance with the worth of wild lands, which was of great service to him. He was also engaged to a considerable extent in shipping. At his death his fortune was valued at several hundred thousand dollars. As the agent of the Pejepscot Company, whose claims were not very readily acknowledged, he was often brought into unfriendly relations with the squatters, who were numerous in Maine at that time, and several adventures of his are handed down by tradition, laughable enough, were it not that his life was oftentimes really endangered. His influence and popularity were almost unlimited in his native town of Newbury, which he represented in the General Court for nearly thirty years in succession. His children were : —

    I. Michael, born 14 March, 1772 ; died 16 March. 1830.

    II. Edward, born 12 March, 1773 ; died 21 Sept., 1849.

    III. Alice, born 1 Feb., 1775 ; died 27 July, 1819.

    IV. Sally, born 16 Jan., 1777 ; died 26 Dec., 1777.

    V. Sarah, born 27 July, 1779 ; died 12 March, 1868.

    VI. Moses, born 17 Aug., 1781 ; died 7 March, 1802.

    VII. Anna, born 29 Nov., 1783 ; died 13 Nov., 1866.

    VIII. Mary, born 4 May, 1786 ; died 26 Jan., 1871.

    IX. Judith Toppan, born 5 Sept., 1788 ; died 16 April, 1791.

    X. Josiah, born 13 Jan., 1791 ; died 5 Feb., 1860.

Michael graduated at Dartmouth, 1792 ; married, 19 Oct., 1800, Sarah Stover, who died 28 July, 1801. His second wife, Elizabeth Ricker of Somersworth, whom he married Feb., 1802, survived him, dying 18 March, 1864, in her 88th year. He had but one child : —

    I. Josiah Stover, born 9 July, 1801 ; died 2 April, 1862.

ON. JOSIAH STOVER, graduated at Bowdoin, at the head of the celebrated class of 1825. He was President of the Atlantic and St. Lawrence Railroad, and Speaker of the Maine House of Representatives for several years. He married Abby Chamberlain Sept., 1833. Their only child was : —

I. Abby Isabella, born 27 Nov., 1834.

Abby Isabella was married to Col. Charles Benjamin Merrill of Portland, 24 Sept., 1856. Col. Merrill was born April, 1827, graduated at Bowdoin in the class of 1847, and at Harvard Law School in 1849. He studied and practised law in Portland for several years. In July, 1862, he was commissioned Lieutenant-Colonel of the 17th Maine, and served with distinction in the late war, being a participant in the battles of Fredericksburg, Gettysburg, Orange Grove, and Chancellorsville, where he was particularly complimented for his valuable services. Their children are : —

I. Josiah Little, born 1 Feb., 1859 ; died 24 Aug., 1859.

II. Mary Southgate, born 8 April, 1861 ; died 29 Aug., 1861.

III. Isabella Little, born 5 April, 1862.

IV. Charles Putnam, born 18 Sept., 1864.

V. John Fuller Appleton, born 10 Feb., 1866.

VI. Daniel Chamberlain, born 10 Jan., 1868; died 20 April, 1868.

VII. Alec Boyd, born 19 Feb., 1869; died 26 June, 1869.

VIII. Richard King, born 21 June, 1871; died 28 July, 1872.

HON. EDWARD [Josiah Moses] graduated at Dartmouth College in 1797; married 10 Jan., 1799, Hannah, daughter of Capt. Thomas Brown of Newbury. She died 1 Aug., 1828, aged 56 years. His second wife, Hannah, widow of Tappan Chase of Portland, whom he married 21 June, 1831, survived him, and died 14 June, 1868, aged 78 years.

He studied law in the office of Judge Parsons in Newburyport; practised his profession for several years with considerable success; was county attorney and publisher of law reports for the Commonwealth. After the destructive fire of 1811, by which he lost nearly all of his property, he removed to Portland, and in 1826 to Auburn, where he continued to reside during the remainder of his life. The owner by inheritance of the larger part of the surrounding territory, he had great influence in directing and promoting the growth of the place. It is needless to say that this power was always exerted in the right direction. One of his first acts was to establish and endow an academy, which continued in successful operation for forty years, and attained a high reputation throughout the State. After the rise of the high-school system the grounds and a portion of its funds were transferred by the trustees to the town, which now maintains an Edward Little High School, and is soon to erect a statue in his honor. His children are:—

I. Thomas Brown, born 4 Nov., 1799; died 7 March, 1854.

II. Josiah, born 29 April, 1801; died 9 Aug., 1865.

III. Sarah, born 29 Oct., 1802; died 14 Jan., 1810.

IV. Hannah, born 25 Feb., 1804.

V. Edward Toppan, born 13 Sept., 1805; died Nov., 1805.

VI. Maria, born 22 Oct., 1806; died 22 Feb., 1817.

VII. Eliza, born 20 Sept., 1808; died 19 Oct., 1809.

VIII. Edward Toppan, born 29 Dec., 1809; died 5 Nov., 1867.

IX. Sarah, born 18 May, 1811.

X. Moses, born 24 June, 1812; died 18 July, 1812.

XI. Moses, born 5 July, 1813; died 2 Dec., 1813.

HOMAS BROWN[7] [Edward Josiah[5]] was one of the first and most active of the business men of Auburn, deacon of the Congregational Church for several years, and Commissioner for Cumberland County. Married, 7 Feb.,1820, Eunice Thrasher of Portland, who died at Auburn 9 April, 1844, aged 46 ; and 8 Jan., 1845, Mrs. Fanny Barker Towne, who survives him. Their children are : —

    I. Maria, born 11 Feb., 1821 ; died 25 Dec., 1867.

    II. William Robison, born 20 May, 1822 ; died 15 March, 1872.

    III. Sarah Toppan, born 16 March, 1824 ; died 29 Nov., 1828.

    IV. Hannah, born 30 April, 1826 ; died 5 May, 1844.

    V. Thomas Spencer, born 31 Dec., 1827 ; died 15 Feb., 1847.

    VI. Sarah Toppan, born 16 Feb., 1829 ; died 21 April, 1832.

    VII. Caroline Robison, born 7 April, 1831 ; died 18 Sept., 1853.

    VIII. Mary Brewster, born 17 Dec., 1832 ; died 29 Oct., 1868.

    IX. Eunice, born 20 Aug., 1834; died 11 Feb., 1853.

    X. Ellen Thurston, born 8 May, 1836.

    XI. Henry, born 21 Dec., 1838.

XII. Sarah Hale, born 4 Aug., 1840; married William K. Eminger 27 Sept., 1865; died 16 May, 1871.

XIII. Fanny Barker, born 17 Dec., 1845; died 13 March, 1851.

XIV. Frances Caroline, born 19 Dec., 1853.

Maria[8] [Thomas[7] Edward[6]] married 21 Oct., 1840, John Herrick, who died 9 July, 1856, aged 40. Their children are :—

I. Maria Augusta, born 1 Aug., 1841; died 7 Aug., 1870.

II. Lydia Thompson, born 10 Feb., 1845; married Capt. Lester Dwinel of Bangor 7 Dec., 1870.

III. Eunice Thrasher, born 21 March, 1847; died 9 Sept., 1865.

IV. John Little, born 3 Jan., 1854; died 23 March, 1855.

Maria Augusta Herrick[9] was married to John S. Adams, eldest son of the Rev. A. C. Adams, 25 Aug., 1864. Their children are :—

I. Kate Leland, born 21 Jan., 1867.

II. Nellie Little, born 10 April, 1869; died 10 May, 1869.

III. Maria Herrick, born 23 July, 1870; died 17 Aug., 1870.

William Robison⁸ [Thomas⁷ Edward⁶] married, 21 Dec., 1843, Rachel Dunning Thompson. Children:—

    I. Henrietta Maria, born 15 June, 1844.

    II. Hannah, born 15 Aug., 1845.

Hannah⁹ married, 8 June, 1868, Frank C. Shaefer. Their children are:—

    I. Frank William, born 13 June, 1869; died 4 July, 1873.

    II. Thomas Little, born 2 Aug., 1871.

    III. Henrietta Little, born 13 Aug., 1873; died 25 March, 1874.

Caroline Robison [Thomas⁷ Edward⁶] was married, 2 June, 1852, to Hon. Charles W. Goddard, then of Auburn, who was born in Portland 29 Dec., 1825; graduated at Bowdoin College 1844. Their only child was,

    I. Benj. Little, born 8 Aug., 1853; died 23 Jan., 1854.

Mary Brewster⁸ [Thomas⁷ Edward⁶] was married, 27 Feb., 1856, to Roscoe Barrell, who died 4 Oct., 1861, aged 29. Their children are:—

    I. Thomas Little, born 21 Aug., 1857.

    II. Caroline Robison, born 3 April, 1859.

Henry⁸ [Thomas⁷ Edward⁶] married Mary E. Simmons, daughter of E. W. Simmons of Portland, 5 June, 1867. Was member of famous 1st Maine Cavalry, in thirty-six engagements; was on three raids under Stoneman, Kilpatrick, and Sheridan ; and wounded at the battle of Sheppardstown, Va. In 1868 appointed Postmaster of Auburn, Me., which office he held two terms ; has been reappointed a third. Their children are : —

    I. Mary Simmons, born 28 April, 1868.

   II. Thomas Brown, born 2 Feb., 1870 ; died 24 July, 1871.

  III. Caroline Robison, born 21 Jan., 1876.

OSIAH[2] [Edward[6] Josiah[5]] was educated at Bowdoin, studied law with his father, practised his profession for several years, afterwards engaged in trade and manufactures. Married, 2 Sept., 1822, Mary Holt Cummings of Norway, Me., who died at Minot, 6 Oct., 1829, aged 25 years, 6 months ; 30 March, 1830, Nancy Williams Bradford, who died in Auburn 20 Nov., 1834, aged 26 years and 7 months ; 26 May, 1835, Sally Brooks of Alfred, born 3 May, 1807, who died at Auburn 15 April, 1849, aged 41 years and 11 months ; and 20 May, 1850, Charlotte Ann Brooks, born 26 Dec., 1817, who survives him.

After an absence of many years he returned to his native place, Newburyport, where he continued to reside until his death. As a man of business he possessed excellent judgment, was exact in all his dealings, and persevering in the prosecution of his plans. As a citizen he was the firm friend of good order and good morals, and took a deep interest in all measures affecting the well-being of the community in which he lived. He was for many years a member of the Christian church, and hearty in his support of Christian institutions and ordinances. In the summer of 1865 he was one of a company of gentlemen of Newburyport who chartered the schooner Martha May for an excursion along the coast of Maine. Aug. 8 the company arrived at the head of Some's Sound, Mt. Desert. Early in the morning, Aug. 9, not feeling well, he went up on deck, and just as day was breaking suddenly fell and expired. His remains were taken to Auburn for burial. His kindliness of manner, his ready sympathy, his improving conversation, made him a favorite with all. His children are : —

    I. Elizabeth Mary Todd, born in Lewiston, Me., 24 Sept., 1823.

    II. Edward, born in Lewiston, 25 June, 1825.

    III. Francis Brown, born in Minot, Me., 20 June, 1827 ; married, 4 Oct., 1854, Maria Warren Brooks of Dorchester, Mass., who died in Chicago 19 Oct., 1874.

    IV. Mary Cummings, born in Auburn, Me., 19 Feb., 1831 ; died 18 Sept., 1831.

    V. Josiah, born in Auburn, 10 Sept., 1832.

    VI. Charles Jenkins, born in Auburn, 9 April, 1836.

    VII. George, born in Auburn, 26 May, 1837 ; died 23 Aug., 1838.

VIII. Nancy Bradford, born in Auburn, 11 Aug., 1838; died at San Francisco, 17 April, 1873.

IX. Horace Chapin, born in Auburn, 14 Jan., 1840.

X. George, born 10 Feb., 1841; died 1 May, 1842.

Elizabeth Mary Todd[8] [Josiah[7]] was married at Lewiston, Me., 14 Oct., 1847, to George H. Ambrose, born in Concord, N. H., 22 Jan., 1825.   They live in Chicago, Ill.   Their children are : —

I. Mary Cummings, born in Auburn, Me., 11 Oct., 1848 ; died 14 Sept., 1875.

II. George Francis, born in Auburn, 27 April, 1851.

III. Chas Edwd, born in Cordova, Ill., 23 Oct., 1855.

IV. Josiah Little, born in Amboy, Ill., 16 Sept., 1857.

V. Elizabeth, born in Chicago, Ill., 20 Nov., 1865.

Mary Cummings[9] [Elizabeth[8] Josiah[7]] married, 27 Oct., 1870, Alexander Fleming Stevenson of Chicago, who was born at Hamburg, Germany, 8 April, 1837.

Col. Stevenson came to this country in 1854, studied law with Judge Wilkinson of Rock Island, and was admitted to the bar in 1859.   At the beginning of the late war he entered the army as 1st Lieut. in the 42d Illinois Volunteers, and was appointed at the battle of Stone River Inspector-General on the Staff of Gen. P. H. Sheridan ; served two terms as a member of the State Legislature from Chicago, and was elected in 1869 Clerk of the Superior Court of Cook County.   Their children are : —

   I. Alexander Francis, born 1 May, 1872.

   II. Mary Louise, born 30 June, 1875.

Edward [Josiah] married, 8 Oct., 1856, Julia Williams, born in Dixfield, Me., 5 May, 1830, daughter of C. L. Eustis of Auburn, Me. Their children are : —

   I. Fannie Eustis, born in Amboy, 10 March, 1858.

   II. Francis Cummings, born in Chicago, 20 July, 1865.

Josiah [Josiah Edward] married, 17 Nov., 1859, Mary A. D. Hussey, born at Belleville, Ohio, 10 Aug., 1835. They live at Amboy, Ill. Their children are : —

   I. Josiah, born 12 Oct., 1860.

   II. Nancy Jane, born 19 Sept., 1862.

   III. Mary Elizabeth, born 16 July, 1864.

   IV. Edward Hussey, born 21 June, 1866.

   V. Maria Warren, born 17 Feb., 1871.

Charles Jenkins [Josiah Edward] married, 30 Dec., 1858, Harriet Antoinette Chamberlin, who was born at Jewett City, Conn., 2 April, 1839. Their children are : —

   I. Charlotte Brooks, born in Portland, 29 March, 1863 ; died in Yarmouth, Me., 25 Feb., 1867.

   II. Grace Chamberlin, born in Yarmouth, Me., 15 Dec., 1867.

   III. Infant son, born in Yarmouth, Me., 10 Sept., 1869 ; died 12 Sept., 1869.

Nancy Bradford[8] [Josiah[7] Edward[6]] married, 13 Nov., 1861, Francis S. Spring of San Francisco, born in Newburyport, Mass., 14 May, 1829.   Their children are:—

    I. John Hopkins, born 13 Dec., 1862.
    II. Francis Vergnies, born 8 July, 1864; died 30 Dec., 1871.
    III. Charlotte Brooks, born 30 July, 1866.
    IV. George Lewis, born 22 May, 1869.
    V. Horace, born 4 Sept., 1870; died 5 Sept., 1870.

Capt. Horace Chapin[8] [Josiah[7]] married, 1 Nov., 1860, Rosa J., born at Auburn 6 May, 1843, daughter of Jacob H. Roak of Auburn.   He entered the army during the late war, and was elected Captain of Co. B, Twenty-third Maine Infantry, which was mustered into the service 29 Sept., 1862.   He subsequently resigned on account of ill-health.   Their children are:—

    I. Nellie Roak, born in Portland, 15 Aug., 1861.
    II. Nancy Brooks, born in Auburn, 8 Oct., 1864.
    III. Jacob Roak, born in Lewiston, 30 June, 1870.
    IV. Charlotte Brooks, born in L., 12 Feb., 1872.
    V. Rose, born in Lewiston, 1 April, 1873.

ANNAH[7] [Edward[6] Josiah[5]] married, 2 Aug., 1832, Samuel Pickard, Esq., of Auburn, who died 2 Nov., 1872, aged 79 years and 8 months.   Mr. Pickard was born in Rowley, Mass., 9 March, 1793.   The early years of his life were spent in teaching in his native town, which he also represented in the Legislature. By his first wife, Sarah Coffin, a sister of Joshua Coffin, the historian of Newbury, who died in 1831, he had four children: Josiah Little, Superintendent of Schools in Chicago, graduated at Bowdoin College in 1844; Joseph Coffin, late Principal High School of Milwaukee, Wis., and now Professor at State Industrial University, Urbanna, Ill., graduated at Bowdoin College in 1846; Samuel Thomas, one of the proprietors of the Portland Transcript; Daniel Webster, graduated at Bowdoin College in 1848; was pastor Congregational Church, Groveland, Mass.; died 1860. In 1832 Mr. Pickard removed to Lewiston, where he entered into business. He early became treasurer of one of the manufacturing companies, a position which he held until his death. He was interested in the cause of education, served as Trustee of the Bangor Theological Seminary, and Overseer of Bowdoin College. Their children are:—

I. Sarah Little, born 4 May, 1833.
II. Edward Little, born 25 Dec., 1834.
III. Charles Weston, born 28 Oct., 1836.
IV. George Henry, born 2 April, 1838; graduated at Amherst 1858; died while studying for the ministry, 16 March, 1863.
V. John, born 21 April, 1840.   [Feb., 1868.
VI. Horace Chapin, born 24 Dec., 1841; died 21

VII. Frederick William, born 7 Oct., 1843; died 4 Oct., 1844.

VIII. Hannah Brown, born 13 Sept., 1845; died 4 Sept., 1865.

IX. Mary Little Hale, born 28 Jan., 1849.

Sarah Little Pickard⁸ [Hannah⁷ Edward⁶] married, 16 May, 1867, Hon. Peter F. Sanborn of Hallowell, Me.   Their children are : —

I. Samuel Pickard, born 18 Aug., 1868.

II. Joseph Appleton, born 24 Dec., 1870; died 12 Aug., 1871.

III. Stanley Hale, born 16 March, 1873; died 28 June, 1874.

Edward Little Pickard⁸ [Hannah⁷ Edward⁶] married, 25 Dec., 1856, at Bangor, Me., Fannie Maria, daughter of Joshua Coffin Plummer, Esq.   Their children are : —

I. Julia Maria, born 9 Feb., 1858.

II. Samuel Webster, born 20 Aug., 1859; died 31 July, 1865.

III. Fanny Dix, born 23 June, 1862; died 1 Sept., 1862.

IV. Charles Dix, born 9 Nov., 1864.

V. George Plummer, born 3 Aug., 1867.

VI. Edward Little, Jr., born 15 Feb., 1870.

VII. Augustus Bishop, born 31 July, 1873; died 31 July, 1874.

Charles Weston Pickard [Hannah Edward] graduated at Bowdoin 1857 ; married, 12 March, 1862, Henrietta Eliza Groth, adopted daughter of Hon. Josiah L. Pickard of Chicago. Their children are :——

    I. George Henry, born 21 Oct., 1863 ; died 27 Jan., 1868.

    II. Frederick William, born 2 Sept., 1871.

John Pickard [Hannah Edward] married, 23 Oct., 1862, Anna Elizabeth, daughter of James Downs, who died 5 Sept., 1864, aged 27 ; and Mary Adeline Leavitt 28 May, 1868. His children were :

    I. Samuel Henry,   died 26 July, 1864.

                      } twins, born 18 May, 1864.

    II. Hannah Elizabeth,   died 1 Aug., 1864.

Horace Chapin Pickard [Hannah Edward] married, 14 Sept., 1859, Sarah Sawyer. His only child was,

    I. Florence Valentine, born 14 Feb., 1861 ; died 7 Sept., 1865.

Mary Little Hale Pickard [Hannah Edward] married, 2 Aug., 1869, Woodbury K., son of Luther Dana of Portland. Their children are :——

    I. Louisa Woodbury, born 27 April, 1870.

    II. Hannah Little, born 1 Aug., 1872.

    III. Philip, born 3 Aug., 1874.

    IV. Ethel, born 25 July, 1876.

DWARD TOPPAN[7] [Edward[6] Josiah[5] Moses[4]] studied law with his father, represented his town in the State Legislature for several years, and was Judge of Probate for Androscoggin County. He was also for many years a Director of the Maine Central Railroad and of the First National Bank of Auburn. His reputation as an upright and able lawyer is somewhat strikingly shown by the fact that a term of court rarely passed without some case being referred to him for decision. He married, 2 Oct., 1839, Melinda C., daughter of the Rev. W. B. Adams. who died at Auburn 30 Sept., 1842 ; and 9 June, 1846, Lucy Jane, daughter of Zeba Bliss, who survives him. Their children are : —

I. Edward Adams, born 13 May, 1841 ; died 14 April, 1876.
II. Weston Tappan, born 17 April, 1842 ; died 26 Aug., 1865.
III. George Thomas, born 14 May, 1857 ; graduated at Bowdoin College in the class of 1877.

Edward Adams[8] [Edward T.[7] Edward[6]] was a prominent and successful business man, a Director of the First National Bank of Auburn, and a Trustee of the Savings Bank ; also served in the City Council. He married, 6 Sept., 1864, Susan Maria Jordan, daughter of William Jordan of Danville, Me. Their children are:—

I. Edward Toppan, born 17 May, 1866.

II. Horace, born 3 Oct., 1868.

III. Mabel, born 6 May, 1872.

SARAH[7] [Edward[6] Josiah[5]] married, 30 Sept., 1841, Charles Clark, Esq., who received the appointment of United States Marshal for Maine from President Lincoln, fulfilled the duties of the office for two terms with great success, and has held several other responsible positions. Their children are : —

I. Sarah Caroline, born 17 March, 1846 ; died 15 Aug., 1846.

II. Charles Edward, born 8 July, 1850 ; graduated at Bowdoin 1871 ; studied medicine at Harvard Medical School.

ALICE [Josiah[5]] married Thomas Hale of Newbury, 25 May, 1797. Their children were : —

I. Rev. Benjamin, D. D., born 23 Nov., 1797 ; died 15 July, 1863.

II. Moses Little, born 7 April, 1799 ; died 22 June, 1874.

III. Thomas, born 13 Oct., 1800 ; died 28 May, 1854.

IV. Sarah, born 29 March, 1802 ; died 9 April, 1834.

V. Josiah Little, born 9 Dec., 1803; died 26 Feb., 1875.

JOSIAH L. HALE entered the office of the Merchants Insurance Co. of Boston at the age of 18, where his fidelity and courteous manners soon won him promotion. In 1825 he became Secretary of the Washington Marine Insurance Co.; and in 1828 — on the opening of a branch office — he went to New York as its manager. After a year of marked success in this position, he joined with the late Walter R. Jones in establishing the Atlantic Insurance Co. of New York. To do this he had to raise $150,000 of the capital stock; and his Boston friends proved their confidence in his character and ability by subscriptions to twice that amount.

In this position he remained for 25 years, in which time the company became the leading marine insurance company in the country. He was compelled by continued ill health to resign his office in 1854. In the Resolutions of respect and regret then adopted the Trustees refer to the company as "established essentially through (his) active instrumentality, and (as having) under his administration enjoyed a course of uninterrupted success."

Mr. Hale held with an intelligent and firm conviction the great doctrines of grace; but without bigotry or sectarianism. The Bible was his daily companion, and doing good his constant delight.

VI. Edward, born 8 Nov., 1805.

VII. Mary, born 5 July, 1807 ; died 13 March, 1859.

VIII. Dr. Ebenezer, born 28 April, 1809 ; died 2 Aug., 1847.

IX. Alice Little, born 15 April, 1811.

X. Capt. Joshua, born 14 Dec., 1812.

Mary [Josiah] married Thomas Hale of Newbury, 17 Sept., 1822. Their only child was : —

I. James White, born 8 Sept., 1827, and died 11 Oct., 1832.

REV. BENJAMIN HALE, D. D., graduated at Bowdoin College in 1818, studied theology at Andover, was Professor of Chemistry and Mineralogy in Dartmouth College, President of Hobart College, Geneva, N. Y., for over twenty years, and the author of various educational works. He married, 9 April, 1823, Mary Caroline King. Their children are : —

I. Caroline Alice, born 16 Aug., 1826 ; died 9 Feb., 1837.

II. Benjamin, born 31 Oct., 1827.

III. Mary King, born 3 April, 1830 ; died 28 Dec., 1838.

IV. Sarah Elizabeth, born 3 July, 1832.

  V. Thomas, born 11 July, 1834.
  VI. Cyrus King, born 17 March, 1838 ; died 5 June,
    1874.
  VII. Josiah Little, born 1 April, 1841.

Benjamin Hale graduated at Hobart College 1848 ; married Lucy B. Hale, 29 Oct., 1855.   Their children are : —

  I. James White, born 12 June, 1858.
  II. Mary Alice, born 6 March, 1873 ; died 8 Aug.,
    1873.

Sarah Elizabeth Hale was married to the Rev. Malcolm Douglas, D. D. of Andover, 14 Oct., 1851.   Their children are : —

  I. Charles Edward, born 11 Sept., 1852 ; died 13
    Sept., 1852.
  II. Mary Caroline, born 19 Oct., 1853.
  III. Benjamin Hale, born 29 Dec., 1855.
  IV. David Bates, born 14 Aug., 1858.
  V. Malcolm, born 25 Nov., 1864.
  VI. Andrew Ellicot, born 5 July, 1867.
  VII. Moses Hale, born 29 July, 1870.

Thomas Hale graduated at Hobart College 1853 ; Vice-President Pacific Mutual Insurance Company ; N. Y., married Lucy F. Searcy 24 Feb., 1870.   Their children are : —

I. Charlotte Elizabeth Prescott, born 5 Dec., 1870.
II. Thomas, born 4 Feb., 1874.

Cyrus[8] King Hale graduated at Hobart College 1858,
d Harvard Law School 1860; married, 9 May, 1866,
ice Little, only child of Capt. Joshua Hale. Their
ildren are: —

I. Cyrus King, born 24 Jan., 1867.
II. Joshua, born 8 May, 1869.
III. Josiah Little, born 24 Nov., 1870.
IV. Benjamin, born 6 May, 1873.

Dr. Josiah Little Hale graduated at Hobart College
60, studied medicine at Harvard Medical School
d in Europe; married Annie Skinner Pierce 24
ril, 1873. Their children are: —

I. Josiah Little, born 6 March, 1874; died 16
April, 1874.
II. Mary Dean, born 15 March, 1876.

Moses Little Hale, an eminent business man of

Thomas[7] Hale married Caroline Charlotte Jordan, 3 Oct., 1836. They had no children.

Edward[7] Hale married widow Elizabeth L. Brown 30 Jan., 1837. Their adopted daughter Ellen F., wife of E. R. Sibley of St. Louis, Mo., died at her father's residence, Newbury, Vt., 12 Nov., 1869.

Dr. Ebenezer[7] Hale graduated at Dartmouth 1829; married Sarah W. Bannister 13 June, 1844. They had one child : —

    I. Ebenezer, born 8 Oct., 1845; died 19 Feb., 1860.

Alice[7] Little Hale married, 23 April, 1832, Rev. John Charles March, pastor of the Belleville Church, Newburyport, who died 26 Sept., 1846. They had two children : —

    I. James White Hale, born 5 Sept., 1834; died 27 Oct., 1838.
    II. Sarah Hale, born 19 Dec., 1836; died 8 Oct., 1837.

Capt. Joshua[7] Hale married Sophia Cutler Tenney 4 Jan., 1844. Their only child is : —

    I. Alice Little, born 27 Aug., 1845.

Sarah[5] [Josiah[3] Moses[4]] married, 18 Nov., 1801, John Little of Campton, N. H., who died June 30, 1856. Their only child, an infant son, was born and died 26 Dec., 1802.

Anna[6] [Josiah[3] Moses[4]] married, 10 March, 1804, William Atkinson.   Their children are : —

I. Joseph, born 28 Aug., 1805 ; died 15 Oct., 1805.
II. William, born 11 Oct., 1806 ; married Adeline Reed 1829 ; died 15 Nov., 1862.
III. Charles, born 18 May, 1808 ; married Eliza Ann Bates in 1830.
IV. Joshua Toppan, born 9 April, 1810.
V. Joseph, born 15 Feb., 1812.
VI. Dr. Moses Little, born 27 July, 1814 ; died 18 Jan., 1852.
VII. Judith, born 25 June, 1817.
VIII. Rev. George Henry, born 10 May, 1819.
IX. Josiah Little, born 14 Feb., 1823, and married, in California, Isabella Clarkson, 4 July, 1854.

Joshua Toppan[7] Atkinson married Emeline Little in 1832.   Their children are : —

I. Anna Elizabeth, born 26 Nov., 1836 ; married Edward Payson Kyes of Newbury, Vt., 3 Nov., 1863.

II. James William, born 26 May, 1839; married Sarah Savage 3 June, 1874.

III. Sarah Little, born 28 May, 1842.

IV. Josiah Little, born 18 Dec., 1845.

V. George Little, born 23 Dec., 1848; died 23 March, 1876.

Joseph[7] Atkinson married Charlotte Swasey in 1836, and Frances Farrington 4 June, 1851. Their children are:—

I. William Hazen, born 19 Oct., 1838.

II. George L., born 28 May, 1842; died 9 Aug., 1860.

III. Charles M., born 13 Aug., 1845.

William Hazen[8] [Joseph[7] Atkinson] married Ella Maria Hibbard 11 Jan., 1865. Their children are:—

I. Charlotte, born 19 Jan., 1867.

II. Frances Maria, born 23 Aug., 1871.

Dr. Moses Little[7] Atkinson graduated at Dartmouth 1838; married Catherine M. Bartlett 7 May, 1845. Their children are:—

I. Edmund Bartlett,   died Nov., 1847.
                         } twins, born 6 May, 1846.
II. William,   died Aug., 1846.

III. Edmund Bartlett, born 25 Dec., 1848.

IV. Martha W., born 6 Jan., 1851.

Judith[7] Atkinson married Gideon D. Dickinson 18 May, 1837. Their children are : —

   I. Anna Caroline, born 6 May, 1838 ; married William D. Hawley 9 Sept., 1862 ; died 7 Dec., 1862.

   II. Mary L., born 9 Aug., 1841.

Mary L. Dickinson [Judith Dickinson[7]] married Charles H. Deere 9 Sept., 1862. Their children are : —

   I. Anna Caroline, born 20 Aug., 1864.

   II. Katie M., born 16 Oct., 1866.

Rev. George Henry[7] Atkinson graduated at Dartmouth in 1843, and at Andover Theological Seminary in 1846. Married Nancy Bates of Springfield, Vt., 8 Oct., 1846. Their children are : —

   I. Sophia Blake, born and died 12 Sept., 1848.

   II. George Henry, born 16 Sept., 1849 ; graduated at Dartmouth 1871, and Long Island Medical School 1875.

   III. Annie Sophia Bates, born 24 Oct., 1851.

   IV. Edward Moses Little, born 23 Dec., 1854 ; graduated at Pacific University 1876.

   V. Sarah Frances, born 11 Nov., 1856 ; died 18 Oct., 1860.

VI. Charles William, born 11 Dec., 1858 ; died 27 Aug., 1859.

Anna Sophia Bates[3] Atkinson [Rev. George H. Atkinson] married Frank Manly Warren of Portland, Oregon, 8 Oct., 1872.   Their children are :—

I. Frances Elizabeth, born 7 Sept., 1873.
II. Frank Manly, born 25 Aug., 1876.

JOSIAH[5] [Josiah[5] Moses[4]] graduated at Bowdoin in 1811 ; was an extensive land-owner, and engaged in manufactures ; a member of Maine Historical Society, and an Overseet of Bowdoin College, where he established a professorship of Natural Science ; founded Newburyport Public Library ; married, 24 Jan., 1814, Sophronia Balch, who survived him, dying 24 June, 1872.   They had no children.

Abigail[5] [Moses[4] Moses[3]] married John Gideon Bailey of Newbury, Vt.   At her death, 20 Sept., 1838, she is said to have had 350 descendants.   Her children were :—

I. Sarah, born 25 Nov., 1765 ; married James Bailey.
II. James, born 17 Aug., 1767 ; married Miss Stevens.

III. Elizabeth, born 29 Jan., 1770 ; died Dec., 1788.

IV. Moses Little, born 1772 ; married Elizabeth Dennis of Marblehead.

V. Abigail, born 25 June, 1774 ; married Sumner of Dalton, N. H.

VI. Anna, born 12 May, 1776 ; married, 26 Sept., 1793, Isaac Duffs.

VII. John, born 17 Aug., 1778.

VIII. Prudence, born 13 Nov., 1780.

IX. Daniel, born 27 Sept., 1782 ; married Hannah Hibbard.

X. Josiah Little, born 28 May, 1786 ; married Nancy Carter.

XI. William Wigglesworth, born 12 May, 1788.

XII. Elizabeth Maria, born 26 Nov., 1789 ; married Simon Blake.

XIII. Mary Follansbee, born 28 Jan., 1793 ; married McAlvin.

Lydia [Moses Moses] married, 4 Oct., 1770, John Atkinson of Newbury, who died 1811. Their children were : —

I. John, born 25 June, 1771.

II. Theodore, born 3 April, 1773.

III. Anna, born 25 June, 1775 ; married, 2 June, 1795, Stephen, son of Abner Little.

IV. Lydia, born 4 June, 1777.

V. Moses, born 17 April, 1779.

VI. Joshua, born 4 Feb., 1781; died 5 Feb., 1781.

VII. Judith,   died 10 July, 1782.
             } twins, born 30 April, 1782.

VIII. Abigail, } married Benj. Currier; died 13 Aug., 1811.

IX. Hannah, born 22 Dec., 1784; died 14 Sept., 1833.

X. Joshua, born 29 Jan., 1787; died 29 May, 1792.

XI. Jacob, born 24 March, 1789; married Elizabeth, daughter of Moses Little; died 14 June, 1859.

XII. Josiah Little, born 17 Oct., 1791.

Elizabeth[5] [Moses[4] Moses[3]] married, 24 Nov., 1774, Lieutenant John Carr, son of Robert Carr of Carr's Island, who was afterwards lost at sea. Their only child was : —

I. John, born 4 June, 1778.

After the death of her first husband she married, 20 March, 1783, William Wigglesworth, son of the Rev. Samuel Wigglesworth of Hamilton, who died 26 July, 1786. Their children were : —

I. William, born 27 Dec., 1783; married Sarah Howe; died 1867.

II. Samuel, born 5 Jan., 1786.

Mary[5] [Moses[4] Moses[3]] married, 13 Dec., 1775, Matthias Plant Sawyer, who died Aug., 1777. They had but one child : —

    I. George, born 10 March, 1776.

After the death of her first husband she married, 13 Sept., 1779, Joshua Follansbee of Salisbury, who died Aug., 1821. They had no children.

Hannah[5] [Moses[4] Moses[3]] married, 25 July, 1781, Dr. Moses Sawyer. Their children were : —

    I. Matthias Plant, born 11 July, 1788 ; died 31 March, 1857.
    II. Hannah, born 14 Feb., 1793 ; died 30 May, 1801.
    III. Joseph, born 16 Dec., 1794.

After the death of her first husband she married, July, 1807, Col. James Furnham of Portland, who died in Boston 15 May, 1842, aged 80 years. They had no children.

HON. MOSES [Moses[4] Moses[3]] married 6 Aug., 1786, Elizabeth, daughter of Shubael Dummer, who died 22 Oct., 1840. He held the commission of Justice of the Peace fifty years, represented the town of Newbury in the Legislature nineteen years, was a member of the convention for altering the Constitution of Massachusetts, and a deacon of the Belleville Church for thirty-six years. His children were : —

  I. Abigail, born 13 Oct., 1787; died 14 May, 1871.
  II. William Dummer, born 15 Jan., 1789 ; died 20 Jan., 1868.
  III. Elizabeth, born 23 May, 1792; died Oct., 1856.
  IV. George, born 17 May, 1794 ; died 1856.
  V. Moses Parsons, born 14 Feb., 1796; died 9 Nov., 1865.
  VI. Albert, born 14 Aug., 1800; died 6 Dec., 1852.
  VII. Annie Mary, born 4 Dec., 1803; died 31 March, 1842.
  VIII. Maria, born 4 Jan., 1806.

William Dummer[6] [Moses[5] Moses[4]] married Caroline Stevens, who died in 1873.   Their children are : —

  I. William Dummer, born 1 Aug., 1827 ; married Judith Newhall 26 Dec., 1867.
  II. George F., born 22 Dec., 1829 ; died 1852.
  III. John Gardner, born 5 Oct., 1832 ; married Carrie M. Balch 23 Nov., 1868.
  IV. Mary Bishop, born 15 Sept., 1836.

Mary Bishop[7] [William D.[6] Moses[5]] married, 26 Sept., 1866, Preston Newhall, who died 21 April, 1867.   Their only child was : —

I. Preston, born 8 Aug., 1867; died 20 Sept., 1870.

Elizabeth[6] [Moses[5] Moses[4]] married, 1826, Jacob Atkinson. Their only child is:—

I. Lydia Elizabeth, born 23 Dec., 1831; married Augustus K. Cole 1849. Their only child, Jacob Atkinson, was born 28 July, 1850, and died 11 June, 1854.

George[6] [Moses[5] Moses[4]] married Jane Stone. Their children are:—

I. Jane, born 7 Nov., 1825; died 22 May, 1840.
II. Elizabeth, } died 9 Dec., 1852.
      twins, born 30 Sept., 1827.
III. Abigail B. } married Hutching Eames; died 5 March, 1852.
IV. George, born Sept., 1834.

Moses Parsons[6] [Moses[5] Moses[4]] married, 19 April, 1832, Jane W. Russell. Their children are:—

I. Emily Frances, born 8 May, 1835.
II. Moses, born 1 Dec., 1837; killed by Indians, 13 June, 1866, near Fort Moharè, Arizona.
III. Horace E., born 8 Oct., 1845.
IV. Jennie Russell, born 19 April, 1856; married, 30 Nov., 1875, Francis B. Jones.

Emily Frances[7] [Moses P.[6] Moses[5] Moses[4]] married,

28 May, 1864, Major Charles E. Compton.   Their children are : —

    I. Charles Ludington, born 28 Feb., 1865 ; died 26 July, 1865.

    II. Paul, born 1 Aug., 1866.

    III. Florence, born 20 June, 1870.

Horace F.[7] [Moses P.[6] Moses[5] Moses[4]] married Meribah Underwood, 20 June, 1869 ; lives in Buffalo, N. Y. Their children are : —

    I. Carrie Russell, born 24 Oct., 1870.

    II. Horace, born 24 Dec., 1872.

    III. Charles Compton, born 1 Dec., 1874 ; died January, 1875.

    IV. Emily Compton, born 12 July, 1876.

Anna Mary[6] [Moses[5] Moses[4]] married, 1 June, 1829, Dr. Adams Moore of Littleton, N. H.   Their children were : —

    I. Maria Little, born 11 Oct., 1830 ; died unmarried, 8 July, 1854.

    II. Isabelle McClary, born 24 Nov., 1833 ; married Edwin P. Green of Akron, Ohio, 31 Dec., 1855 ; died 13 March, 1869.

    III. Elizabeth Adams, born 29 May, 1837 ; married Edwin P. Green 25 May, 1870.

IV. Williams Adams, born 27 March, 1842 ; killed
    at the battle of Fredericksburg 13 Dec., 1862.

Maria [Moses Moses] married, 16 Aug., 1843, Dr.
Adams Moore of Littleton, N. H.   Their children
are : —

I. Anna Mary, born 15 April, 1844 ; died 15 April,
   1844.
II. James White, 11 Dec., 1846 ; married, 2 April,
    1874, Caroline E. Granger.

APPENDIX.

———◇———

[Copy of a letter in the possession of Dr. Josiah L. Hale of Boston.]

NEWBURY PORT, June 26th, 1775.

COL. MOSES LITTLE, Cambridge.

SIR:

Prior to other business I must congratulate you on your late good Fortune in the Battle in Charlestown, and the Character your first military Action has obtained. It might look like Flattery to express my Sentiments on the occasion, therefore defer it till I see you, which I hope will be in due Season.

I cannot help dropping one Hint that occurs to my Mind on the Method of securing your Entrenchments, that is, whether they would not puzzle the Enemy in a near Approach if some of the young Locusts & Cedar Trees in the neighborhood were laid at a proper Distance without the Entrenchments to scratch the Shins of the Regulars, and impede their Advance. But this I submit, as being one of the least in Military Knowledge.

Will you permit me to recommend to your very particular attention Stephen Jenkins, in Perkins Company, who was not used well in his late Appointment. I think him very deserving and doubt not youll find him so. If any Opportunity to advance him it will oblige many of his Friends here who are worthy. But this I do not ask if you find him not worthy, nor would I ask it if I thought him so.

You have my best & hearty Wishes for Health & Preservation. May the God of Armies shield you in the Day of Battle and return you safe to your Friends crowned with Honors.

I am

Your particular Friend

Excuse Haste.   & most hble Serv.

TRISTRAM DALTON.

[Copy of a letter in the possession of Mr. J. G. Little of Newburyport.]

NEWBURYPORT [No date].

MOSES LITTLE, ESQ.

SIR,—Agreeably to your request and as far as my memory will serve I will relate my experience in the regiment under the command of your late father in June, 1775. On the morning previous to the engagement of Bunker Hill those of our regiment that were together, were ordered to parade on the common at Cambridge. About 12 o'clock Col. Little came on horseback and ordered us to march to the hill. When we got to Charlestown neck the enemy were throwing shells and firing from their ships and floating batteries to prevent our passing. The Col. rode ahead and ordered us to follow, single file. A cannon ball went between us as we passed and struck a large stone. We marched to the rail fence on the hill and then halted a little while. A part of our Reg't went to the fort and engaged and checked the enemy there twice. The third time he got in among us and we ran out of the fort down hill as fast as we could. While running to the other hill I found that I had one or two cartridges and stopped to use them. While priming a ball struck my right arm above the elbow. I loaded my gun but found no strength in my right arm, then took my gun in my left hand and ran again. In the fort the person on my left was shot down. After we got off we collected our company together and found 9 wounded and 2 missing. viz. Samuel Nelson killed, Jonathan Norton wounded and carried into Boston (where he died). Wounded, Joseph Whittemore, Amos Pearson, Isaac Howard, Joseph Mitchel, William Pray, Aaron Davis, Patrick Harrington, William Elliot, and Daniel Lane.

From your most obt. servant,

AMOS PEARSON.

[Extract from a letter dated Newburyport, 21 June, 1775. Probably written by John Bromfield to Jeremiah Powell. Taken from Massachusetts Historical Society's Proceeding. 1869–1871.]

Mr. Little of Turkey Hill (who I have heard is lately made a colonel) show'd great courage and marched with those under his command, thro' two regiments of our men who were looking on at a distance but were afraid to advance. he set them an example, it seems they did not chuse to follow — he proceeded till he found our people retreating from the Hill being overpowered by numbers. He cover'd their retreat and got off without much loss. He narrowly escaped with his life, as two men were kill'd one on each side of him and he came to the camp all bespattered with blood.

[Copy of a bill in the possession of Mr. J. G. Little of Newburyport.]

DR. *The United State of America* To *Moses Little*, on Express from Gen¹. Bayley To His Excellency Gen¹. Washington, being 350 miles from Coos to Morristown, Feb. 28, 1781.

To my Expenses on the road to head quarters   .   .   946S *

BY THE NAME OF LITTLE.

CPSIA information can be obtained at www.ICGtesting.com
Printed in the USA
BVOW03s1236120615

404417BV00018B/210/P